Silver Investing

(The Definitive Bible)

Why in 2015 the time for silver is now and how to get rich

Table of Contents

Introduction

Silver is a transition metal which is famous for its shine, reflectivity and high industrial usage. It is extracted from various ores and has always caught the attention of many people around the world because of its attractiveness. It has a few unique properties which makes it an important element in the world. The metal is not just shiny and attractive; it is one of the best electrical and thermal conductors and has one of the highest reflectivity indexes amongst all metals. This is the reason why silver is widely used in many industries such as in electronics, photography and in currencies.

Given the worth of the metal and the high demand from industry, investors are now turning their heads in the direction of silver. Many investors are now looking to explore the opportunities that the silver market offers. Since the metal is usually currently available at a cheap cost, an investment in this market is expected to bring positive gains to investors for the short and long term.

What makes Silver particularly interesting though is the *rate* at which industry is starting to use the metal. Early indications are showing that due to limited supply of other suitable metals silver may likely be the next commodity to boom.

Investment is not everyone's cup of tea, however. Not all of us are equipped with the wit and the skills which are required to negotiate a fair and profitable deal. Just like every investment requires a great deal of information, investment in silver too demands high skills and knowledge. While the experienced investors usually have no issue in expanding their investments in the silver market, it is usually the beginners which face problems in gaining profits from their investments.

If you are a new investor or an old one, who wants to gain sufficient knowledge of investment in silver, this is the right place for you. This book contains all the necessary information which you would require as an investor to gain profits out of your deals. Thus read the chapters, follow the tips we have mentioned and enjoy huge sums of money from your investments.

Chapter 1: An overview of Silver Investing

Ask people about the places they have invested their money in, and you would mostly hear them say real-estate, shares or gold. You would rarely come across a person in your circle who would have invested in silver to earn additional income. Well, if you come across such a person, make sure you follow his investment related advices because he is probably wiser than the ones who have invested in gold and currency. You will shortly know how beneficial investment in silver can be for you, your business and family.

Precious metals have always caught the attention of many people. They have been used as money in early times while women have adorned themselves from the jewelries of precious metals. While gold tops the list of the most attractive precious metal for investment, silver is no less than gold. In fact, apart from being used in variety of other useful purposes, silver is now widely used in investment. People are now more inclined towards investing their money in silver rather than gold. This change in investment is because of the numerous benefits that silver offers over gold and other precious metals.

Buying silver or dealing with silver is one of the safest options out there when it comes to investment. This is because silver does not depend upon the operations of the central bank which makes it less controlled as compared to other metals and investment options. The silver market, although a little volatile at times, can offer you safe returns and easy investment. Thus, if you are thinking to invest your money in a safe place, silver investment is your way to go. Let us see some more benefits that this useful metal can offer you in terms of investments.

Not a risky investment

One of the most dreadful situations for an investor can be to see the markets getting crashed. There are a number of investment markets where the investors are left with little to no money when the markets hit their rock bottoms. This is not the case with the silver market though. Although silver markets have seen ups and downs in the past few years just like other markets, once you have the ownership of the metal, you can never be in the losing side. Even if the market crashes, the metal will still have enough value to give you good returns. Thus, it is a less risky investment option which you should add to your portfolios to diversify your risk.

Easy to find low prices of silver

While other financial markets can sometimes make it difficult for the investors to purchase at an appropriate low price, the stability of the silver market means that if you want to purchase the metal, you would be able to spot a low price to purchase easily and make returns out of the investment with ease.

Variety of options

Another good benefit of investment in silver is that you will have a lot of options to choose from while investing your money. So you cannot just buy silver coins, but can also invest your money by purchasing silver jewelry and bars. You may also invest your money in a mutual fund which deals with silver. And if you are wondering if you could get these investment options with ease, let us tell you that purchasing silver is not a big task and you would easily find these options near your area.

These are some of the benefits the metal would offer if you choose to invest your money in the silver market. The metal holds great value in the sense that it is widely required by the industries and can still offer you some very good returns if you invest your money in it. The price of the silver is also not quite high as compared to other metals, although it can still experience some ups and downs occasionally. The low price of the metal, around $40 - $50 an ounce, offers you another advantage of earning high returns by investing less money as compared to other metals.

Thus, if you have extra money to invest, silver market is a wiser choice to opt to. You would end up being richer than your friends in the future who have invested their money in other assets. You might be surprised to know that the major players of the world's wealth, including Bill Gates, are also silver investors. Hence, you could increase your wealth too if you follow their paths and invest in silver.

Chapter 2: Where to Buy and Sell Silver

All the benefits of investing in silver mentioned in the previous chapter can only be availed if you make the best decisions when it comes to investing in silver. While you may find a lot of options to purchase silver, you will not be able to get a good return unless you choose a good dealer and understand the various sizes and purities of silver available with them.

The first way to start your investment is to find a good dealer from whom you can purchase silver bullions and coins at a relatively lower price. However, this task is not an easy one as there are a number of dealers out there in the market who gain extra profit by tricking the investors. Thus, when you go out to buy silver, make sure you keep in mind the following tips:

Do not believe the TV ads of the stores

Stay away from the stores which offer you silver coins and bullions with just 1-2% extra charges through their advertisements. The advertisements are usually deceiving as the stores do not charge extra amount on the face value of silver but on their overall business costs. Thus, 1% or 2% extra money charged on the high business costs can make the silver pretty costly for you. You must always visit the store and find out about the additional charges yourself instead of believing the TV ads.

Stay away from firms with low BBB ratin

A low Better Business Bureau (BBB) rating means that the firm does not have a good reputation when it comes to selling the metal. Thus, avoid these firms at all costs and only buy from stores with better ratings.

Do not buy from a store which does not offer fresh silver

It is fresh silver which has a higher worth. Thus, if you buy silver with even a little scratch on it, there are chances that you might end up selling it at a discount without any profits. Make sure you properly check the silver purchased, and avoid the stores which fool people by selling scratchy coins or bullions.

Always look for a store which is reputable and authentic with better BBB ratings. You may also purchase silver online through good online stores. Apart from the information regarding the stores however, there are a number of other dos and don'ts which you should consider when buying and selling silver.

Do understand the forms of silver

Understanding the type of silver available in the stores is important as it will help you understand the factors which determine the worth of the form of silver and how much should you pay for it. There are various types of silver bars including:

Bullion bars

Bullion bars are the silver bars which are traded on the basis of the silver contents. They mostly contain around 99.5% pure silver and are available in different shapes and sizes. These bars are usually sold at the spot prices or a little above them. Hence if you go to a store which is selling bullion bars at a much higher price than the spot rate, then avoid buying from the store at all costs.

Art bars

Art bars are the silver bars on which some images are crafted. Because of the extra adornments on the art bars, they are a sold at a little higher price than the spot price. However, if you are indifferent between buying a simple silver bar and a crafted one, you must go for the simple ones as with a simple silver bar, you will get a higher amount of silver in the price you are willing to pay for an art bar.

Do know the sizes of silver bars

Apart from the forms of silver bars, it is important that you understand the sizes in which the bars are available to make an informed decision. You should know the price of the silver per ounce in the market so that when you go out to purchase silver, you can easily calculate the expected price according to the size and detect if the store is selling you at an unreasonably higher price. You must also try to purchase the bars in a bulk amount as bulk buying often reduces the overall cost of investment.

Do consider other forms of silver

While it is advisable that you purchase physical silver, you should also look for investments in non-physical options such as silver ETFs and silver certificates. These assets can give a high return too.

Do not get attracted to new silver

While it is true that fresh and new silver out of the mines has its own charm, it does not usually give a higher return just because of its newness. Also, it is often noticed that old but fresh silver is traded more than the new bar out of the mine. It is mostly the silver contents which make the bar more valuable so make sure you focus more on the silver contents when purchasing or selling silver.

Chapter 3: Different Types of Silver

To be able to make the most out of your investments in silver, you should be aware of the common types of silver available. Various types of silver exist in the market because the original silver element is soft and malleable and thus cannot be used in the making of hard jewelry and ornaments. To make it stronger, silver alloys are created with different proportions of the metals such as copper. Hence, you should know the amount of silver contained in each type of silver bar because the bar will be traded according to the value of the silver it contains.

Here are some common types which you might see in the market:

Sterling Silver

The type of silver which is closest to the original metal is sterling silver. It is one of the most precious types of silver because of its high silver contents. Sterling silver consists of minimum 92.5% pure silver and 7.5% other metals. It is mostly copper which is mixed with pure silver to make it stronger and durable. Sterling silver is popular in the world not just because of its high silver contents and strength but also because of its attractive appearance. You would also often hear this type being called the .925 silver. This is to denote that the sterling silver should at least contain 92.5% pure silver metal. Although it has high worth compared to other types, a disadvantage of sterling silver is that it can get tarnished in the long run. This type is also soft because of its high silver contents, and hence cannot be used to make hard materials. Investment in this type of silver is easy and profitable though. Because of its high worth, you would hopefully end up earning good returns if you trade sterling silver. You would not need a high amount to invest in the type of silver and you can also purchase jewelry of sterling silver and then trade it when the prices are favorable.

German Silver

German silver is deceiving in the sense that it does not contain pure silver in it. All it is made of is nickel, copper and zinc. These three metals join together to produce a strong alloy which is similar to the original silver. The alloy has a yellowish color though which makes it easier to distinguish between the original silver and the silver-like-alloy. Despite being an alloy, German silver has properties similar to that of silver. It is used to make things like hard construction materials and strong hospital equipments. Investment in silver is also not hard as this type can easily be found in different stores in the form of bullions and bars. The low price and the high worth and strength make this type a good investment option.

Oxidized Silver

The disadvantage of pure silver is that it cannot be exposed to oxygen and should be regularly cleaned to keep the tarnish at bay. To overcome this issue, silver is exposed to oxygen and pressure where the silver gets tarnished and oxidized. The benefit of getting the silver oxidized is that the oxidation will reduce the likelihood of the metal getting tarnished. You will then have fewer issues in ensuring that the metal stays clean and attractive. Because of the oxidation, the color of the metal gets darker, though it still retains the attractiveness. The darker color does not reduce the value of oxidized silver to a great extent and you can still enjoy high gains from the purchase and trade of this type of metal. Hence, buy a suitable form of the oxidized silver from your nearest stores or through an online store and enjoy huge returns from your investment.

Silver Plating

Another good way to achieve the attractiveness of silver while still ensuring affordability is to electroplate a base metal with silver. The obvious advantages of silver plated metals are that the beauty of the metal rises and you can enjoy beautiful silver-plated ornaments and jewelries at low cost. Although not a preferred choice when it comes to investment in silver, it would still offer you good gains if you choose to trade a silver-plated metal. Just make sure you know that the electroplating will not last forever and the base metal will get exposed at one time or the other.

Apart from the famous four types mentioned above, there are many other types of silver available in the market, each containing unique amounts of silver and other metals. One such example is the Argentium silver which is a type of sterling silver with germanium and copper in it. The amount of silver is still 92.5%, but the addition of germanium reduces the chances of tarnish, and hence, the price of the silver rises. It is difficult to distinguish between sterling silver and Argentium silver just through their appearances. Therefore, make sure you purchase them only through reliable stores so that they do not trick you into selling sterling silver instead of Argentium silver at a higher price.

To sum up, knowledge of the various types of silver available is extremely necessary for all you investors out there since the price of the silver varies with the amount of silver each type contains. You must know the amount of silver in each type to avoid getting fooled by some stores.

Chapter 4: Premium and Spot Silver Pricing

Now that you know the types and forms of silver to buy and sell, it is important that you know the two famous pricing strategies that you would see in the silver market. Both of them have their own benefits and harms, but are nevertheless used extensively to sell and buy silver.

Premium Pricing

One such pricing strategy is premium pricing, in which the prices of a good are kept high to give an impression to the customers that the good is of a higher quality. Although it is not necessary that the good will always be of a higher quality, the higher price makes it easy to separate a particular good from a group of similar goods. Since this pricing strategy singles out a particular product, it is often called skim pricing.

Prices are also kept higher than the usual market prices in order to cover the costs of the sellers while ensuring a reasonable profit from the sales. Through this pricing strategy, the sellers try to maximize their gains through a product for which the consumers are willing to pay more. The strategy is widely used in the corporate world where the firms also utilize premium pricing techniques to improve the image of a brand in the market.

When it comes to silver investment, premium pricing is used by the brokers who want to reduce their risk of losing money in silver investment. This is done by keeping a fair premium on the prices of silver so that even if the prices go down when they are about to sell the silver, the additional premium charged could still give them enough gains in the deal.

This technique, however, cannot be used in every situation. You could only adopt this strategy of pricing when your product has no substitute and there are barriers to entry in the market. This technique is also used by firms which hold patents for certain goods or for the goods which are considered to be worthy and luxurious. Hence, premium pricing is largely used in the silver market because it does not have an equally attractive substitute available and it also holds high value in the eyes of the consumers.

Spot pricing

Another pricing strategy is the spot pricing, which is the current price of a good or a commodity. Spot prices tell you the standard prices you should pay for a good at that particular point in time. Spot prices of silver are calculated using the usual supply and demand laws, and hence they keep on changing as the demand and supply change. Premiums are then charged on the spot prices by the individual dealers according to their costs and risks.

Both types of pricing strategies are important and have a few drawbacks. If we talk about spot pricing, it is an extremely important pricing strategy as it tells you the current value of the good. It is through the current spot prices that the investors hedge their risks and practice derivatives. Spot prices also helps the investors see the minimum standard price that they have to pay for silver and other commodities. Premium pricing, on the other hand, has the advantage of giving the dealers a fair amount of profits on their deals. It also prevents the entry of competitors in the market, and helps the good stay worthy.

Silver is mostly priced on premium, so you should always look for the spot price per ounce of silver and the price the dealer is offering to calculate the premium charged per ounce. Then add the shipping costs and other overhead charges to see which dealer is offering the same amount of silver in low cost. Dealers usually charge a premium to cover their costs and to minimize the risk of losing money, but you should always be wary of the approximate costs the dealers can have to check if they are charging unreasonably high premiums.

On the other hand, you must not always go for the lowest premiums charged as low premiums can sometimes result in low quality silver or a poor service from the dealer. Hence, always look at the reputation of the dealer in the market and see if they are charging fair premiums over spot before investing in silver.

Chapter 5: Silver Storage Techniques

Once you purchase the silver from a good dealer, it is important that you keep it safe and protect it from damage and tarnish. Storing silver and caring for it is a necessary step which, if missed, can cause a lot of trouble for you.

Tarnish

One big problem that comes with silver is that it gets tarnished when it is exposed to air and humidity. It interacts with the oxygen in the atmosphere and gets yellowish and brownish in color. This not only makes the silver less attractive, it also reduces its value. Tarnished silver will obviously be sold for less value and you will have to bear losses on your investment. Hence make sure that you prevent the silver you have bought from getting tarnished by following the tips mentioned below:

Gently clean your silver with soap and water and dry it out using cotton cloth.

To minimize the damage, **wear gloves** before touching your silver.

Do not store your silver in newspapers or cardboard boxes as they increase the likelihood of tarnish.

Cover the metal with a **tarnish-resistant cloth** and then put it in a **polythene bag**.

It would also be good if you also put a **silica gel sachet** near the storage space as it absorbs the sulfides in the air and prevents silver from getting tarnished.

Ensuring safety of silver

Silver is a precious metal which attracts the eyes of the thieves and burglars. If you have invested heavily in the metal and have bought a good amount of silver at home, then you must keep it safe. You need to keep your silver bars and coins in a place where you could prevent it from theft. Here are a few tips to ensure that your silver stays safe.

Store your silver in **third-party vaults** if you are not sure of keeping it safe at your home.

Investment in silver is a private affair which should be **kept secret**. Avoid telling everyone about how much silver you have bought and try not to store the metal in the banks. Storing it in the bank will also let the metal gain a lot of attention.

If you have decided to keep the silver at home, keep them safe in **tarnish-resistant boxes.** Then store the boxes in a place where nobody can find them except you.

It would be wise if you **do not store the boxes in traditional places** like cupboards and safes. Thieves would go straight to these places if they enter your home.

Try **storing them in creative places** like under the ground and within the walls. It would be hard for anyone to guess that you can keep your silver boxes in these places.

Keeping the silver safe should be your first priority if you do not want to bear heavy losses on your investment. Always store them in a secure place in your home and regularly clean the bars to prevent damage and tarnish.

Chapter 6: Why Silver is better than Gold for Investment

The talk of silver versus gold has always been a hot topic of debate among the investors. Since both metals are precious and valuable, investors are always in a state of confusion when it comes to investment in metals. Both gold and silver have their own advantages and drawbacks, and we cannot say for certain that one is better than the other.

In previous years, investors preferred gold over any other metal because of its high worth. Gold is considered more luxurious and is present in much greater quantity than the silver. However, recent trends have shown that many investors now prefer silver over gold because of the advantages that silver offers. Let us look at some of the advantages which you will get if you invest in silver instead of gold.

Silver is cheaper than gold

When it comes to investment, you do not just have to look at the possible returns you will get, but also at the cost that you will have to incur with the investment. It would not be wise to invest in something which costs you a lot of money but cannot promise good returns. Fortunately, this is not the case with silver. If you analyze the prices of gold and silver over the years, you will see that gold prices have usually been much higher than the prices of silver.

While the prices of gold are in thousands, the prices of silver are around 40-50 dollars per ounce. This means that you can have a lot more ounces of silver in the price at which you will get just one ounce of gold. Can you now see how profitable the investment will be? More ounces of silver at lower price would mean even greater returns than gold. This is one of the biggest reasons why investors now prefer silver over gold. What else can be better than low cost and high returns?

Silver's worth is expected to rise in the future

According to the analysts, silver is expected to do well than gold in the upcoming years. This has to do with the demand of both metals. You all must know how important gold is for us, and that the demand of the metal is usually high. However, if we compare the demands of gold and silver, the demand of silver is greater than the demand of gold.

Silver has more applications than gold, making it an important metal in the eyes of investors. It has many industrial uses and is widely used in the sectors such as electronics and photography. It is no hidden fact that the demand of silver has always been greater than the supply of the metal. This trend will continue to rise as silver is irreplaceable and cannot be reused once it is utilized in the industries. This is not true for gold, however, which keeps on circulating from one hand to the other and is rarely destroyed in the process.

Given the increasing demand and the limited supply, the prices of silver will increase in the future. Thus if you invest in silver today, with the added advantage of cheap cost, you will end up earning high returns by selling your silver in future. This advantage is not expected from the investment in gold.

Another advantage that silver has over gold is that silver is **less affected by the economic and financial crisis** as compared to gold. This can be seen from the recent global financial crisis, where the prices of silver rose even though the world was going through tough times.

To sum up, investment in silver is a wise decision as compared to investment in gold. Many investors are now investing their money in silver instead of gold and are earning huge profits. If you too want to earn high gains at cheaper cost, you too should invest your money in silver at your earliest possible convenience.

Chapter 7: Avoiding Silver Scams

Investment in silver, or in any other metal for that matter, is not easy and one has to keep his eyes open to be wary of the possible scams. When every other person is looking to maximize his or her gains, there are chances that some people might cheat you to earn higher profits. Hence, you must be careful when you step in the market to buy silver. Here are some of the things which you should be careful about.

Avoid pooling in the money or buying a certificate

It has always been advised that the investor should take physical possession of silver as it is more worthy and valuable. On the other hand, when you pool in the money to buy silver, the silver is not entirely yours. It belongs to every other member of the pool which can create problems for you in the future.

This is especially true if you pool in to buy silver and store it in the bank. The bank will keep everyone's silver in one place and use the metal if it faces bankruptcy. That is, if the bank goes bankrupt, it will use your silver to pay off its debt and stabilize itself. You will then be compensated with currency, which would obviously be of a lower value than the metal you had stored. Hence, your investment will be gone forever if you pool in the money to buy silver and store it in a bank.

Thus, if you find anyone asking you to invest in silver through this method, run away from them. They are tricking you into a world of problems and losses. You must always try to get physical possession of the metal and keep it as secret as you can.

Avoid buying numismatics

Numismatics is ancient coins and bars which are sold at a higher price because of their rareness. While it is always a pleasure to get your hands on rare and ancient things, it is not a wise option if the sole purpose of buying numismatics is to sell them at a higher price. This is because the coin loses a significant percent of its value when it is resold in the market.

Prices of such rare coins are high because they contain the premiums, the costs of dealers and the additional charges of being a rare commodity. It would have been a good investment option if you could sell a numismatic coin at an even higher price. However, this does not happen as the price of such rare coins are already so high that it becomes difficult for people to re-sell these coins at higher prices. Not many investors are interested in buying such rare coins at high prices and therefore you would incur losses on your investments.

Therefore, whenever you go out to buy silver, avoid buying numismatic coins no matter how much the dealer forces you to buy them. The dealer will also tell you how these coins will not be confiscated by the government and how you can earn high profits out of these valuable coins. However, none of it is true. These coins have equal chances of being confiscated by the government and you will not be spared just because of possessing antique coins.

Stay away from leveraging, future and options

A leveraged investment is one in which you invest in silver through loans. Leveraging is a technique which is employed by many investors who want to maximize their gains. They borrow money from banks and other financial institutions, buy silver from that money and resell it at a higher price to gain profits. The more they borrow and invest, the higher the gain. However, everything is not as sweet as it seems to be. Leveraging comes with a lot of risk which can be difficult to manage by amateurs and professionals both.

Consider a situation where you have borrowed a lot of money from the bank at a reasonable interest rate, but you fail to gain profits on your investment. Without the profits to pay off the loan, your life will be in much trouble. You can easily go bankrupt if the leveraging technique does not work out for you. Hence if you want to stay away from trouble and want to practice risk free silver investment, stay away from borrowing money to finance your investment. Never listen to someone who advises you to borrow money from them, no matter how appealing their advertisements look. Always earn your own money to invest in silver as it is through this way that you can be a lot more certain of earning high returns.

Futures and options are two other techniques which the investors use to maximize their gains by setting the contract date in the future when the price is expected to be favorable. This technique is like leveraging too which involves a lot of risk. Stay away from futures and options especially if you are a new investor.

Apart from these three basic scams, you must be wary of the dealer too who can often trick you into charging higher prices by giving nothing valuable in return. Silver scams can be found everywhere in the market and you must stay cautious to avoid bearing losses.

Chapter 8: Uses for Silver which make it good for Investment

Silver is a precious metal whose worth cannot be fully explained in a few words. It is a valuable element whose shine, reflectivity and high conductivity are used in a variety of industries. From being used by women in their jewelries to being used by photographers in making films, silver helps us in a wide variety of ways. It is because of the usefulness of the metal, coupled with cheap cost and high returns that the investors now prefer to invest in this metal. Let us look at some of the ways which you investors can use silver for.

Jewelry and accessories

Silver has been used in jewelry and accessories since ancient times. Women of all ages and times have loved the shine and attractiveness that silver jewelry has. Not only does jewelry made from silver look appealing, but it is also economical as the prices of silver are quite low as compared to other precious metals. While gold is also preferred in accessories, silver gains an edge over the gold because of its cheap cost and high attractiveness.

It is mostly sterling silver which is used to make jewelry and ornaments. In most cases, pure silver is also mixed with other metals in a limited quantity to create silver alloys of greater strength. This further increases the strength and appeal of the jewelry. Silver jewelry market is a booming market as the demand for silver jewelry does not seem to decrease. Therefore, if you choose to invest in silver and buy a good amount of the metal, there will always be jewelers out there in the market who will be willing to buy silver from you at reasonable prices.

Table Ware

Just as you would see silver being used in the jewelry, you would see silver around you in your homes on your dinner tables. Some of you might have got tableware and cutlery made form silver, while others might have little table adornments made from silver. Silver is also extensively used to make tableware because of its properties to shine and reflect. Just like silver jewelry, tableware is also made from sterling silver which has copper added in it to increase its strength.

Thus, the demand for silver also comes from the silversmiths who make beautiful cutlery and tableware for your homes. Since many people buy tableware made from silver, the demand of silver is always high, reducing your risk of investment.

Coins

Since it is a valuable element, the governments in ancient times used to use silver to make coins. It was widely used in currencies of various early civilizations, with each empire having its own stamp on the silver coin. Silver coins were also made from sterling silver. It is because of the wide use of sterling silver in currencies that British currency was called pound sterling.

Although silver coins have been replaced by paper money in many parts of the world, the demand of silver coins is still present in some African and South Asian countries. Hence your investment in silver coins will not go in vain as the high demand will make the prices rise in the future, giving you high returns on your investment.

Conductors

Silver being a metal, is a great conductor. It is used in a variety of electrical appliances because of its ability to conduct electricity at a greater speed. In recent times, silver is used as a superconductor in power transmission. This super conductor increases electrical conductivity, thus transmitting the electricity at a greater speed. Silver wires are considered for this job as they also have the advantage of being light in weight and size. This is not all; silver batteries are also used in many electronic tools such as watches and cameras. The presence of silver enhances the performance of an electrical appliance or tool, thus reducing the costs and increasing the productivity. The use of silver as a superconductor makes it even more worthy of your time and money. Investing your money in this metal will not go in vain because of the demand this metal has in the industry.

Other uses

Apart from the uses of silver mentioned above, there are a number of ways in which this metal helps our economy and industries. It is used in **silicon cells,** which is used as a solar cell to generate electricity. Silver is also used in **photography and in mirrors** because of its high reflectivity. Silver is so important for our industries and home that life without it cannot be imagined. This is the reason why the demand for this metal is always high

The increasing demand of the metal because of its extensive use brings in a lot of advantages for the investors. It reduces the risk of losing money as increasing demand and limited supply would continue to increase the price of silver in the future. It not only reduces your risk of losing money, but also increases your gains from investment. Therefore, if you choose to invest your money today in silver, the increase in prices in the future would mean that you can sell your silver at a much higher price and earn a lot of high gains from the deal. What are you waiting for then? Buy silver now and start making huge sums of money!

Chapter 9: How to get Started today!

Now that you know how valuable investment in silver can turn out to be, it is high time that you seriously consider investing your money in the silver market. Since investment is not an easy task, especially for beginners, we have combined a few tips to help you get started today. Follow all the tips religiously and see your investments turning into gains.

Study the spot prices

Spot prices are the current prices of silver in the market. The spot price is the standard minimum price you will have to pay if you decide to invest your money in this market. You will then be charged premiums by different dealers on top of the spot prices according to the costs of the dealers.

In order to successfully manage your portfolios, it is extremely important that you first look at the current spot prices of silver. The information is present on a number of websites through which you can do a thorough analysis and see if the current price is according to your plans and budget. Do not invest in silver at a particular time when the spot price is either too high or too low for you. You must also see the trend of the spot prices in the past few years to be able to predict the spot prices of the future. This will help you make informed decisions.

Another good reason why you should look at the spot prices first is that it helps you see how much premium should be charged by the dealers. Spot prices helps you calculate the premiums charged by different dealers which can then help you in analyzing which dealer to go to. You should always choose a dealer who is not charging high premiums but is still offering great service and high quality silver.

Silver shopping

Once you have analyzed if it is the right time for you to invest in the silver market, look for a good dealer to buy silver from. Always look for a reliable dealer who has a reputation in the market of providing good service to the customers. Your dealer should not charge high premiums in return for a poor service or a low quality or damaged silver. Do not be tempted to follow the attractive advertisements of some of the dealers and do your own research about the dealer before shopping for silver.

Once you have decided which dealer you would go to, choose the type of silver you would like to have. You have a lot of options to choose from. For example you can either buy silver coins or bullions, or invest your money in silver Exchange Traded Funds (ETFs). It is always better, however, to have physical possession of the silver through coins and bullions.

Once you buy silver and decide to store it in your homes, make sure you care for it well and prevent it from any possible theft and damage. Regularly clean your bars and coins using the methods we have described in the previous chapters and make sure the silver does not get tarnished.

Finding Junk Silver

Many of you would take junk silver to be the leftover pieces of silver which are not of any use. Well, this is not what we call junk silver. Junk silver is the name given to the coins which were in use before 1960s. They have high silver contents, as compared to the coins in the present times and are no longer counted as official currency coins by the government – hence the term junk silver.

Junk silver holds tremendous importance for you investors because it offers high silver contents at reasonable prices. The good thing about them is that they are still easily available in any local dealer's shop or on some websites selling silver coins. You may also find these coins in your home, especially if you have an older parent or grandparent living with you.

If you go out and buy junk silver from the market, make sure you do not pay a premium of more than 25%. Junk silver can offer you lots of gains because many investors have not explored this opportunity yet.

Consider silver stock markets

In order to get a good grasp of the ongoing prices of silver in the market, you should look at the prices of silver in the commodity market and exchange. You can easily trade your silver in the stock markets and even indulge in futures and options. You will also get a chance to interact with a number of other experienced investors who might share their experiences with you in this market.

After exploring various options to sell your silver in the stock market or elsewhere, you should get the deal signed with a trustworthy customer who could pay you high enough to cover your costs of investment. You may not be able to gain high profits on your first deal, but once you gain more experience and reputation in the market, money will keep flowing in.

Chapter 10: Advanced Silver Investment Techniques

Investment in silver is not always in the form of coins and bullions. There are many more options through which you can earn money in the silver market. These new options, however, are mostly used by experienced players in the market who have greater trading and negotiating skills. Hence, it is advised that you too should go for these advanced techniques once you have gained enough experience in the market. Let us tell you what these advanced options are.

Silver-Backed Exchange Traded Funds

This is a method in which you buy ETF shares which are backed by physical silver. You trade shares in the stock market but the physical metal does not remain in your possession. It is usually stored in a bank which can use the stored metal in certain circumstances. ETFs do not come with a high cost and you will find this option to be an affordable one.

Futures

This is a technique used by many experienced investors to reduce risk associated with investment. In this method, the seller agrees to deliver the silver at a future date at a price which is decided at the time of deal. Hence investors who feel that the prices of silver will go down in the future will decide the price today according to the current higher prices so that they do not face losses in the future when the prices will be low and the silver will be delivered. This is a risk as well since the price can go either way. If, due to any reason, the prices increase, instead of getting decreased than the investor will incur losses on his deal. This is why you should only indulge in futures if you have gained enough knowledge about how the prices of silver work in the market.

Silver streaming companies

Since silver is usually produced in the process of mining other elements, silver streaming companies provide loans to the miners to mine other metals and give the by-product of silver to them at a low cost. The advantage these silver streaming companies have is that they do not have to invest time, money and resources to mine the metal themselves. However, since they do not possess the mine, changes in demand of silver can alter their profits easily.

Mining companies

Apart from investing money in the shares of silver streaming companies, you can invest money in the shares of mining companies as well whose main product is the silver. These companies, however, are not big enough to give good gains on the shares. They have their own internal problems which can decrease your gains from investment.

These are some of the advanced options that many investors use. Remember that these techniques require high skills and experience and you should not directly make your first investment in these advanced options. Use them later when you have gained a fair amount of experience in the market.

Chapter 11: Further Information and Resources

Investment in silver is a big topic which requires a lot of knowledge and experience. In order to become an expert investor, you need to read a lot about the ways in which the market performs and the tips you can use to maximize your gains from investment. Apart from all the valuable information we have presented in this book for you, you need to go an extra mile and read more if you want to gain more money.

It is for this reason that we have combined a list of resources which we have used in this book, so that you could go over these resources and gain extra valuable information. Remember that the more you read the better investor you will be. Here are the links for your reference. Go through them to become an expert investor.

Book

Get the Skinny on Silver Investing: Contains a full guide on what you need to learn when investing on silver.

https://books.google.com.pk/books?hl=en&lr=&id=T9iQtHlDdjcC&oi=fnd&pg=PP1&dq=overview+of+silver+investing&ots=IPgRTJBlYm&sig=q0zFjvAWqPwEOEEBWS921PV_d-s#v=onepage&q=overview%20of%20silver%20investing&f=false

Blog

Total Return: It has explains options for silver investing

http://blogs.wsj.com/totalreturn/2014/11/11/how-to-invest-in-silver/

Websites

eBay: Learn which is best for you; silver or gold?

http://www.ebay.com/gds/What-is-the-best-investment-silver-or-gold-/10000000115915104/g.html

JMBullion: Learn about spot pricing

http://www.jmbullion.com/investing-guide/pricing-payments/spot-prices/

Smallbusiness.chron: Talks about premium pricing

http://smallbusiness.chron.com/premium-pricing-strategy-1107.html

Conclusion

To sum up, silver is a valuable metal which can give us high returns if we invest our money in the silver market. It offers a number of advantages over other traditional investment options, such as gold, making it an appealing choice over other metals.

In order to maximize your gains from the investment, make sure you keep your eyes open for all sorts of cheating and frauds in the market. Remember to always check the spot prices and compare the premiums of the dealers before buying silver from a particular dealer. Once you have bought the silver, keep it safe in your homes in some areas where the thieves will not find it. Keep your investment a private affair and half of your problems will be gone.

Silver is a precious element whose applications and usage in the industrial sector makes it an important thing to invest money in. Hence, do not waste your time, grab your money and buy silver. Within no time your deals will lead you to great glory and financial success.

Happy investing!